Old NEWTON MEARNS

by

Anne Loudon and David Kidd

The place I knew so well in early days, when it was 'far away', an upland village and parish, a place of dreams, Sir D. Y.

The William Mann memorial fountain originally stood at the south-west corner of Newton Mearns Cross and is now situated at the Ayr Road entrance to the Avenue. In earlier days it refreshed the many walkers and cyclists who passed through Mearns in pursuit of recreation. William Mann (1853–1904) was a businessman associated with the Glasgow warehouse of Mann Byars. He was a philanthropist who was responsible for installing the first piped water supply to the village of Newton. Prior to this time water was obtained from wells. Mr Mann also improved drainage from the village and supported the Temperance cause by surrendering the licence of a public house which he had purchased in the Main Street. He was the first captain of both Eastwood and Pollok Golf Clubs and lived latterly at Whitecraigs House, near Whitecraigs station.

ISBN 1 84033 178 X

The authors' royalties from the sale of this book have been donated to the Children's Hospice Association Scotland.

ACKNOWLEDGEMENTS

The authors would like to thank Ken Melvin, who was responsible in years gone by for copying and printing some of the old photographs included in this book, and who also took some of the more modern photographs. We would also like to express our thanks to Mearns History Group, Maud Devine of the East Renfrewshire Heritage Centre, Duncan Hall (Whitecraigs Golf Club), Ian Forrest (Mearns Bowling Club), Peter Milne (Senior Assistant, Map Library, National Library of Scotland), Dr O'Brien (Archivist, the Mitchell Library), Huw Pritchard (Assistant Archivist, South Ayrshire) and George Heaney. Our particular thanks are due to Andrew Russell, for his encouragement, expertise and exceptional recollection of Newton Mearns' past. We would also like to thank many other local people who share our enthusiasm for and interest in the history of Mearns. The publishers would like to thank Robert Grieves for providing the lower picture on page 35, along with extra information on transport matters.

Pictures on the following pages were taken by John W. Crawford: 1, 4, 5, 7, 8, 9, 10, 15, 21 (both), 22, 23, 25 (lower), 42, 44, 45, 46, 47 (horizontal), back cover. (The pictures on pages 6 and 14 may also have been taken by John Crawford.) Pictures on the following pages were taken by James Anderson MBE: 11, 12 (upper), 31, 32, 34.

THE PUBLISHERS REGRET THAT THEY CANNOT SUPPLY COPIES OF ANY PICTURES FEATURED IN THIS BOOK.

FURTHER READING

The books listed below were used by the authors during their research. None of them are available from Stenlake Publishing. Those interested in finding out more are advised to contact their local bookshop or reference library.

Old Days and Ways in Newton Mearns, A. Boyd Scott, Pickering and Inglis Ltd., 1939

A History of Mearns, J. A. Strang, unpublished manuscript in three volumes available for study at Giffnock library, 1939

Mearns Matters, Lesley Williams, 1987

Mearns The Changing Years, Ella Rae, 1987

'Fairest Parish' – A History of Mearns, Susan Hothersall, Eastwood District Libraries, 1988

Eastwood District History and Heritage, Thomas C. Welsh, Eastwood District Libraries, 1989

The Statistical Accounts: Mearns Parish 1796, 1842, 1951

Mearns Rose Society's *Year Book 1901–1902*

'Gardens of the Parish As I Remember Them' by Alan MacCallum, from Mearns Horticultural Society *Centenary Year Book, 1969*

Twelve Centuries of Christian Witness at Mearns Parish Church, W. A. Walker, 1982

A Brief History of Newton Mearns Parish Church, Robert Hodgins, 1989

Newton Mearns Past and Present, The Newton Mearns and Whitecraigs Committee of the Cancer Research Campaign, 1970

Mearns School 1876–1976 anniversary magazine

Eastwood, Our Heritage, third issue, 1986

INTRODUCTION

Mearns, a village and a parish of SE Renfrewshire. The village, called Newton-Mearns (a name as old as 1306), is pleasantly situated on a rising ground, 410 feet above sea-level, 3½ miles WSW of Busby and 7 SSW of Glasgow. A burgh of barony, with the right of holding a weekly market and two annual fairs, it chiefly consists of a single street on the Glasgow and Kilmarnock highroad, and has a post office under Glasgow, with money order, savings bank and telegraph departments, a branch of the Union Bank, a gas work, a hotel, drainage and water-supply schemes and hydrants in case of fire. Pop. (1881) 900, (1891) 908.

This description of the village of Newton Mearns, known also as the Newton and locally as the Nitton, is taken from the *Ordnance Gazetteer of Scotland*, published in 1893. Life in and around Newton Mearns a century ago was very different from life as we know it today. The Newton Inn stood at Mearns Cross and immediately to its east on the Mearnskirk (Eaglesham) Road was Townhead farm. South of the Cross, Robert Anderson was to open his garage in 1902 and semi-detached villas were to be built in 1904–1906. It was to be another 30 years before a major housing boom took place, but there were already some imposing buildings north of the Cross, including the third Secession Church (built 1836) and Mearns Parish School, which opened in 1876. A new manse had been built in 1866 on the Kilmarnock Road, and next door the architect Alexander 'Greek' Thomson built a fine house, now called Croyland, for his friend John Shields in 1874. At Mearnskirk there was a cluster of houses around the glebe of the parish church, as well as a row of cottages at Gateside (known locally as Thumble Ha') on the Old Mearns Road.

There were a number of mansion houses in the area. Todhill-bank (Todhill) and Crookfur were a short walk from the village, with Balgray, Broom (now Belmont House School), Capelrig, Greenbank, Kirkhill and Netherplace a little further away. The imposing Pollok Castle was at Polloktoun. South of Mearnskirk stood Southfield House, which was purchased by the Corporation of Glasgow in 1913 as a home for pre-tuberculous children. Mearnskirk Hospital was later built on the Southfield estate and was officially opened on 12 October 1932 by the Duchess of York (the present Queen Mother). In the 1990s the hospital grounds were sold and developed as a prestigious residential area. Near Mearnskirk at Hazelden was Hazelden House, of which only the stables exist today. These 'big houses' were remarkable for their fine gardens. In a booklet entitled *Gardens of the Parish as I Remember Them* by Alan MacCallum, published in 1969 to celebrate the centenary of the Mearns Horticultural Society, the garden at Crookfur House is described as having a peach house, a vinery, a fig house, a fernery and a melon house.

During the latter part of the nineteenth century Mearns was a rural parish with about 80 farms. Employment was to be found locally in farming and in the cloth processing works at Netherplace, Tofts and Hazelden. Work was also provided by local quarries, such as North Hillhead, Brownside and Crofthead, and in the smiddies at Eastfield, Polloktoun, Newton and Malletsheugh. The mansion houses required domestic staff and gardeners to maintain them, and there were gasworks at Tofts and Broom.

Trains stopped at Giffnock halt from 1864 (a proper station was subsequently opened), making it practical for those living in Mearns to travel to work in Glasgow. Villagers could either take the horse bus from the Newton Inn (Porter's Inn) at Mearns Cross to Giffnock, or cycle to the station where Mr Anderson (who had founded a coal merchant's business in 1832 in Spiersbridge, and whose grandson was to found Andersons garage in Newton Mearns in 1902) had thoughtfully provided shelter for cycles. Andersons of Newton Mearns, a byword for quality and service for over 75 years, became a major employer in the area in the twentieth century.

Mearns was to change irreversibly as road and rail links improved, and as the area became more accessible it was recognised as a highly desirable place in which to live. In the 1930s speculative and local authority housebuilding resulted in the construction of about 1,600 houses. Bungalows began to appear on either side of the Kilmarnock Road and three groups of shops were built near Mearns Cross, two of which survive, the third having been demolished to make way for the shopping centre, which was opened in 1972. With the advent of war and the austerity which followed, it was not until the late 1950s that housebuilding began again in earnest. In recent years there has been much residential development in the Mearns area, both for the private sector and local authority, so much so that the new Mearns Primary School has recently opened with provision for over 900 pupils.

The village, which was already in decline by the mid-1930s, suffered neglect during and after the Second World War and was largely derelict by the 1960s, when it was purchased by a developer with a view to the construction of a shopping centre. This was later upgraded and renamed The Avenue at Mearns in 1991. It is a popular venue both for those living locally and from outside the area, and could be described as an unofficial community centre.

The demise of the village marked the end point of the gradual transition from what was predominantly a self-contained rural community a century ago to what is today essentially a residential suburb of Glasgow. It seems a pity, however, that the village was allowed to become derelict to the point of no return. In the present spirit of conservation one ventures to believe that modern planners would have greater vision, and that the village of Newton would exist today in the centre of the community.

Newton Mearns Cross was situated on the Kilmarnock (Ayr) Road. This had been completed in 1832 and was originally known as the New Line. The Barrhead Road led west from the Cross, with the Mearnskirk (Eaglesham) Road branching off to the east. Although the Kilmarnock Road subsequently became the focus of the village, with buildings such as Porter's Inn (the white two-storey building, above) and Andersons garage situated on it, the older Main Street lay parallel and to the west of Kilmarnock Road. The aerial photograph on the inside back cover clearly shows Main Street, which at its northern end became continuous with Capelrig Road.

Looking west along Barrhead Road from Mearns Cross, with the end of Main Street visible in the middle distance on the right. Originally the village was composed of weavers' cottages and single-storey terraces, although these were gradually replaced by more substantial two-storey buildings. Some of the buildings acquired fascinating names such as the Marble Arch and the Teapot Close. The former stood on the east side of Main Street and through its entrance a courtyard was reached from where there was access to several dwellings at ground floor level. Stairs led to an open landing from which entry was gained to further accommodation on the first floor and in the attic. The Teapot Close was situated at the north end of the Main Street. One explanation for its name was its proximity to the well at the foot of the Teawell Brae. The water drawn from that well obviously made a good cup of tea!

An early view of the Main Street looking southwards showing thatched weavers' cottages on the left. The Teawell Brae, at the north end of the village, led to Tofts where there was a bleachworks and gasworks. In 1996 Miller Homes reconstructed the well (situated on Greenlaw Road near the junction with Greenlaw Drive) after which the brae was named. Pokehat Brae was the steep hill encountered on approaching the village from Polloktoun (Poketoun). It is thought to have received its name as a contraction of Pollok Halt and is the route along which funerals processed from the west of the parish towards the graveyard at Mearnskirk. In the early days coffins were carried on the shoulders of the bearers who, because of the steepness of the hill, had to halt on the incline in order to rest – hence the name Pollok Halt.

The Doctor's Building (also known as Newton Place) stood on the east side of Main Street and was built on the site of the row of thatched cottages seen in the picture opposite. It was erected by Dr Mackinlay, after whom Mackinlay Place was named. A tree, which stands by the access road to the east of the shopping centre, marks the position of the boundary of the back court of Newton Place and the school yard. Dr Mackinlay's consulting rooms were in the rear of his residence, Firwood House, which still stands on the south side of Eaglesham Road. The doctor established his practice in Mearns in 1880 and built Firwood when he married in 1891. He made his visits in a horse and gig and later in an Arrol Johnston motor car which he drove at five miles an hour! In *Old Days and Ways in Newton Mearns*, A. Boyd Scott writes of the parish 'humming with stories of his [Dr Mackinlay's] secret tenderness, his surreptitious aid, his scorn of money from the poor'. His successor was Dr Fordyce, who served the community with distinction from 1926 until 1974. The sheltered housing complex, Fordyce Court, was named in his honour.

The Newton Inn, illustrated here, was in many ways the focal point of the village. Also known as Porter's Inn (after Thomas Porter who was innkeeper at the end of the nineteenth century), it stood at the Cross on the site of the present Texaco garage. The surgery recently vacated by Dr Quin and partners was built in the inn's yard. In 1842 it was described as a 'good inn', and must have benefited from its position on the New Line, the road south which ran from Nellie's Toll (i.e. Eastwood Toll, the toll-keeper being Nellie Niven) towards Ayrshire, which had been constructed a decade earlier. After the Glasgow–Barrhead railway line was opened in 1848 a coach service ran from the Newton Inn to connect with the railway at Kennishead. When Giffnock halt opened in 1864 a horse bus service connected the inn with the Glasgow train. In this *c.*1908 photograph a funeral procession is assembling at Mearns Cross. Several onlookers are seen at the window of the Newton Inn and the little girl in the foreground is weeping. Andersons garage can be seen in the distance on the right.

The Mearns & Giffnock horse bus photographed at Giffnock station. It is recorded that on many occasions the bus from Mearns had to race to catch the train. There were several train services to Glasgow, and the one which departed about 8 a.m. was said to carry mainly those of 'under cashier rank'. The train at about 9 a.m. apparently carried clerks and cashiers, while the 10 a.m. departure was used by 'governors and ladies'! The station yard at Giffnock is said to have been filled with private carriages meeting the trains twice daily. Mr Anderson, coal merchant, supplied shelter for cycles for the use of those who cycled to the station from Mearns. Whitecraigs station was opened on a branch of the Largs and Ayr railway line in 1903, and Glasgow Corporation Transport instituted a tram service to Giffnock in 1905. These measures facilitated travel for those in Mearns who worked in Glasgow. The horse bus service ceased in 1904 but a charabanc was introduced about 1920.

Looking west along Barrhead Road towards the tenements of Ashview Terrace and the Co-operative building. The first Roman Catholic church in Mearns, St Cadoc's Chapel, was built adjacent to the Co-op in 1906 and extended in 1956. In 1981 the congregation moved to a new church in Fruin Avenue, and the former chapel is now occupied by the Jewish *Habonim Dror*. Ashview Terrace was so-named because it was built on a road lined by ash trees. The Western SMT bus depot (see page 35) was built in 1932 in the field on the right.

The Newton had a 'post office under Glasgow' from 1860. Prior to this time, letters were left at the Newton Inn in the care of the innkeeper. Mr Hector Currie was the postmaster of the post office and sorting office in Barrhead Road. Mrs Currie is pictured in the doorway of the shop with Miss Agnes Scott on her right. An earlier post office was located in the Main Street opposite the Star tearoom.

Prospect House, a three-storey property with extensive gardens, stood at the north end of Main Street on the east side. At the rear of the house was an oriel window from which Singer's clock, a well-known landmark in Clydebank, could be seen and the horror of the Clydebank blitz in March 1941 was witnessed. The police houses at the north end of the Avenue car park were built on the site of Prospect House, one of two large town houses in the Main Street. Hope House, built by Samuel Bringan the grocer, was the other. The lamp-post stands at the top of the Teawell Brae (the present Greenlaw Road), and one of the 'summer seats' is just visible. These seats were a favourite meeting place for village folk, who gathered to 'put the world to rights' and enjoy the marvellous panorama of the hills.

Mr John Russell (who died in 1919) in the garden of Prospect House. This was adjacent to Crookfur Park – now the site of Parklands and of the sports pitch and running track. Mr Russell and his sons and grandsons were all keen and accomplished gardeners. In addition to extensive flower gardens, the garden at Prospect House had large glasshouses and a vinery. Gardening was a leisure activity keenly pursued in Mearns at the beginning of the twentieth century. There were the professionally laid out gardens of the 'big houses', cared for by very knowledgeable and experienced gardeners. Many local folk who were keen gardeners spent what leisure time they had cultivating their allotments known as the Botanics.

Below: It is believed that the Horticultural Society was founded in 1858 after John Russell Snr (facing page) invited some men who were arguing about which of them had grown the best cabbage to bring their exhibits to his joiner's shop for adjudication the following Saturday. Mearns Rose Society was in existence by the late 1890s and continued until the First World War. Neil Russell, brother of John Russell of Prospect House (pictured below with his nephews Andrew (left) and John (right)) was a compulsive rose grower and called his house on the Capelrig Road, Rosegarth. This photograph was taken in the garden of Prospect House and shows the Sir John Reid Trophy, which the Russells had won at the Scottish National Sweet Pea, Rose and Carnation Society exhibition at the Kelvin Hall in 1936. The memorial garden on the Ayr Road outside Mearns Bowling Club was dedicated to John Russell, who was president of the Horticultural Society from 1945 until 1973. In its centenary year Percy Thrower, the well-known TV gardener, opened the flower show.

Above: The flower garden of Prospect House with Crookfur Park in the background. The park was known locally as Crookfur Field and was part of the Crookfur estate. Crookfur House was said to be a 'charming old mansion' and the description of its garden by Alan MacCallum is contained on page 3. Within living memory the house was owned by the Templeton family – a branch of the renowned carpet manufacturing family. Crookfur House was destroyed by fire in the 1950s and in 1960 the 13 acre estate was acquired by the Scottish Retail Drapers Association to build a housing complex for retired drapers. In 1967 the Crookfur Cottage Homes, designed by Sir Basil Spence, were opened by Lady Fraser of Allander.

Samuel Bringan's shop stood on the Barrhead Road near the Cross facing south. Bringan built Hope House, a substantial building in the Main Street which stood next to the Castleview Dairy (known locally as Connell's Dairy). He not only supplied groceries but provided for the needs of the farming community, selling such items as grass seed and seed potatoes. Samuel Bringan owned another shop in East Kilbride. Another well-known grocer in the village was James Bowman, who served his apprenticeship

with Bringan. Following a period of eighteen years during which he was manager of Robert Osborne's grocer's shop, he took over the business in 1916. He won prizes in Glasgow, Edinburgh and London for tea blending from 1922–1924, and in 1931 the council of the Institute of Certified Grocers elected him a Fellow of the Institute in recognition of his skills.

In 1743 the 'United Society' of Mearns, Neilston and Eaglesham built a church and manse in the Main Street. The adherents of the society were nonconformists, often of Covenanting background, and in 1738 they had joined the Associate Presbytery (the Secession Church). This was set up in protest by Ebenezer Erskine following the Patronage Act, which denied church members the right to appoint their ministers. Instead such appointments were to be made at the whim of the patron, the local landowner. This picture shows the former church (foreground) during the latter part of its life when in use as a shop and dwelling. Its frontage was 68 feet wide, and it was unusual in that it had pews and a slate (rather than thatched) roof. The sandstone tenement beyond the church is the Doctor's Building (illustrated on page 7).

Main Street, Newton Mearns

The two-storey manse (with crow-stepped gables) stood next door to the church on Main Street, 290 feet from its junction with the Barrhead Road. At the time of the manse's demolition in 1938 the church building was still in existence. Its first minister, Andrew Thomson, was ordained in the church (called the 'meeting house') on 26 March 1746 – three weeks before the Battle of Culloden.

16

Church politics continued to cause dissent, and in 1747 the newly-formed congregation of the Secession Church became engaged in a dispute concerning the Burgess Oath, an oath demanded of the burgesses of the cities of Glasgow, Perth and Edinburgh. This read as a vow of allegiance to Protestantism but was regarded by some Seceders as a veiled approval of the 'Established Church with all its corruptions'. Mr Andrew Thomson, the minister of the Secession Church, at first supported the so-called Burghers but six months later

declared for the anti-Burghers. By 1749 the Burgher faction were demanding possession of the church. A protracted legal dispute ensued which ended when the full bench of the senators of the College of Justice found in favour of the Burghers, and Mr Thomson and his congregation found themselves without a church or manse. They built a second church and manse in the village, and these were occupied in 1754. Meanwhile however, the Burgher congregation diminished to such an extent that it was no longer able to maintain the original church and manse, and offered them to the anti-Burghers in 1760. They moved back to the original church but declined the manse, preferring their own building (above). In later years this became known as Newton House. The house stood in the vicinity of the north car park of the shopping centre and was demolished c.1967, and when the car park was being constructed the well which had served it was discovered. A third manse (located at 204 Ayr Road and still in existence) was built in 1866.

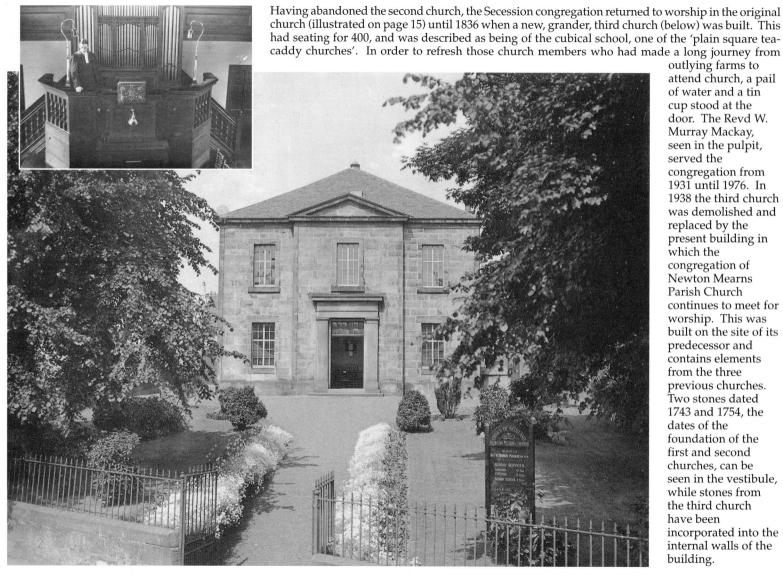

Having abandoned the second church, the Secession congregation returned to worship in the original church (illustrated on page 15) until 1836 when a new, grander, third church (below) was built. This had seating for 400, and was described as being of the cubical school, one of the 'plain square tea-caddy churches'. In order to refresh those church members who had made a long journey from outlying farms to attend church, a pail of water and a tin cup stood at the door. The Revd W. Murray Mackay, seen in the pulpit, served the congregation from 1931 until 1976. In 1938 the third church was demolished and replaced by the present building in which the congregation of Newton Mearns Parish Church continues to meet for worship. This was built on the site of its predecessor and contains elements from the three previous churches. Two stones dated 1743 and 1754, the dates of the foundation of the first and second churches, can be seen in the vestibule, while stones from the third church have been incorporated into the internal walls of the building.

Hazelden Print Works

Cotton spinning was introduced to the west of Scotland in the late eighteenth century. Two cotton mills were functioning at Busby by 1780 and there was another in Eaglesham by 1794. Cotton cloth was cheaper to manufacture than linen, and before long superseded wool and silk in popularity. Raw cotton contained impurities such as colouring matter and seed husks, and further contaminants were incorporated in it during the spinning process. Cotton cloth therefore needed to be washed and bleached. Originally the cloth was laid out in the open, watered several times a day and bleached by the sun. The industry was revolutionised by the invention of chemical bleaching powder, the patent for which was taken out by Charles Tennant in 1799 when working at Darnley (he had previously worked at the bleachfield at Wellmeadow). Following the manufacture of bleaching powder the bleaching process was performed indoors and therefore was no longer weather dependent. Hazelden works (illustrated here) seems to have come into existence as a bleachfield in the 1820s. It had various functions over the century, e.g. calico printing from 1838, and was latterly a silk printing works. According to J. A. Strang, 300 workers were employed there in 1846. Hazelden House is no longer in existence but its stables are in use today as a riding school.

The *New Statistical Account* (1842) doesn't mention Hazelden works, but refers to a printfield at Netherplace, as well as a printfield and bleachfield at Wellmeadow. Known locally as Wallace's after an early proprietor, the Netherplace works (illustrated here) was the best-known of the cloth processing units in the area and was in existence by 1818. In the 1830s it combined with the nearby calico (plain cotton cloth) printing works at Tofts and by the 1860s gave employment to 400, some of whom lived in the village of Newton. The Tofts works, which were demolished in 1930, were located on the Capelrig Burn near the junction of Crookfur Road and Harvie Avenue. A major employer in the district, Wallace & Co. continued in operation until 1980. The plant was reopened in 1986 by the English Sewing Company Ltd. and is now operated by Coats Barber, a company involved in the worldwide industrial thread market.

At Netherplace and the Tofts works there was a hostel for single women known as the 'woman house'. In 1861, 69 boarders were resident in the Netherplace woman house (illustrated here), originating mainly from the Highlands and Ireland. The works' pond, which is believed to date from 1850–1860, is on the left of the photograph. Netherplace House is in the background, partly obscured by trees.

An ample supply of fresh water, engineering advances and the escalating demands of the increasing population of Glasgow all helped to promote the cloth processing industry in Mearns parish in the nineteenth century. There were seven establishments within easy walking distance of Newton: Balgray, Broom, Greenfield, Hazelden, Netherplace, Tofts and Wellmeadow. (Balgray bleachworks, which were already in decline, were submerged when the Balgray reservoir of the Gorbals Gravitation Company (later the Glasgow Corporation Waterworks) was completed in 1854.) According to the 1841 census, 70 workers, many of them immigrants, lived in cottages such as these around the Hazelden works.

A century ago there were 80 farms in Mearns parish, some of which are remembered in modern street names such as Knowes Road, Blackhouse Avenue, Netherton Road and Langrig Road. Mearns dairy produce was much in demand in Glasgow for generations. The *Statistical Account* of 1796 states that 'every farm is stocked with milk cows; and the principal object of the farmer is to produce butter, and butter milk, for the Glasgow market. The butter that is made here, and especially that which is salted for winter's use, is reckoned preferable to any other, and the demand for it is vastly greater than can be answered.' The Shaw farm (illustrated here) was sold *c*.1954 but continued as a dairy until the Shaw Farm flats were built on the site in 1969–1970. The front door of the farmhouse is said to have been taken from the manse of the old parish church at Mearnskirk. This manse was built in 1789 and replaced by the building shown on page 43 in 1842.

Townhead Farm was situated near Mearns Cross on the Eaglesham Road, approximately where the recently vacated doctors' surgery stands and behind the Newton Inn. Its proximity to the village emphasises the rural nature of the community. The entrance to Townhead House is opposite the farm. When the *New Statistical Account* was written in 1842 its author claimed that 'Butter and butter-milk are here manufactured in a style not surpassed in any other district in the west of Scotland . . . the veritable produce of the celebrated dairies of the Mearns'. Milk from local farms was delivered early each morning to the Glasgow dairies, a procession of one-horse carts making the journey between 4 and 5 a.m. Accordingly the road to Glasgow was known as the 'Milky Way'. It seems that it was not uncommon – especially on a Sunday – to see a one-horse milk cart returning from Glasgow at about 10 a.m. with the driver asleep and the horse in charge.

Blacksmiths played an important role in the community in the days prior to the development of motorised vehicles, when horses required shoes and cartwheels regularly needed renewal. The farming community was particularly dependent on the skills of blacksmiths for the maintenance of farm implements. This 1926 picture shows Eastfield Smiddy at Mearnskirk with blacksmith Jimmie Ritchie and his assistant. In addition to Eastfield, there were two smiddies in Newton itself, with further blacksmiths' shops at Polloktoun, Malletsheugh and Waterfoot.

The outhouse adjacent to this familiar restaurant at Mearnskirk was formerly the Eastfield blacksmith's shop. David Cassells (born 1816) established a smiddy at Malletsheugh between 1837 and 1841 and produced innovative labour-saving agricultural machinery. Each implement he produced bore a cast iron Cassells nameplate. A thresher and a potato cutter made by Cassells were still in existence in the late 1980s but sadly can no longer be traced.

The last of the castles of the estate of Over Pollok, Pollok Castle was built in 1886 to replace an earlier building that had been destroyed by fire in 1882. This previous castle was built in the 'Renaissance style' in the late seventeenth century by the first baronet, Sir Robert Pollok de Pollok. Knighted in 1703 for his services at the time of the Glorious Revolution of 1688, Sir Robert (who was largely responsible for the laying out of the estate) had an active political and military career. He became MP for Renfrewshire following the Act of Union of 1707 and was appointed commander of the garrison at Fort William in 1715 at the time of the Jacobite uprising. During the Second World War the castle and grounds were requisitioned by the army and used as an ammunition store. Miss Fergusson Pollok, the last of the ancient family of Pollok to live in the castle, resided in one of its wings until 1944. The castle was demolished in 1954.

Pollok Castle, Newton Mearns

When Captain Thomas Crawford of Jordanhill, a supporter of Mary, Queen of Scots, married a Pollok, the family name became Crawford Pollok. He captured Dumbarton Castle three years after the Battle of Langside, and was given the honour of having the castle depicted on his coat of arms. This coat of arms was inscribed over the door of the East Lodge of Pollok Castle (illustrated here). In addition to Dumbarton Castle it included a boar speared by an arrow, the legend being that a member of the Pollok family killed the last wild boar in the neighbourhood.

Left: Southfield House was demolished in the years following the First World War. The nurses' home was built on the site of the old house, and in 1999 the building firm of John Dickie received a Civic Trust award for their conversion of the building (at Southwood Place) to residential accommodation.

Right: The entrance to Mearnskirk Hospital and the beech avenue which formerly led to Southfield House.

The estate of 'Sufield' (Southfield) is shown on Timothy Pont's late sixteenth century map of Renfrewshire and on Willem Blaeu's Renfroana map published in Amsterdam in 1654. The original feu right of Southfield was granted to John Urie, a solicitor, by Sir Archibald Stewart of Blackhall in 1691. About 1800 the estate came into the possession of the Hutchison family and remained in their hands until the death of Lady Montgomery Cunninghame in 1902.

In 1913 the house and estate were acquired for £17,000 by the Corporation of the City of Glasgow, which originally intended to use Southfield as a 'country home for pre tuberculous children'. Plans in which the mansion house was to be retained as an administrative block were approved in 1915. These plans made provision for 300 beds for children suffering from 'surgical tuberculosis' and for 160 sanatorium beds for adult males. However, with the advent of the First World War, building was delayed and the revised plans of 1919 did not include the house, which by that time was in poor repair.

The new Mearnskirk Hospital opened at Southfield on 9 May 1930, and the first patients to arrive were a group of children from Robroyston Hospital in Glasgow. George McEwan, a six year old patient, proudly presented a large box of cigarettes to the medical superintendent, Dr John Wilson, on behalf of the staff of Robroyston. HRH the Duchess of York, the present Queen Mother, officially opened the hospital on 12 October 1932 and planted an oak tree to commemorate the event. (This tree was inadvertently cut down when the developers moved in after closure of the hospital in the 1990s, much to the disquiet of local people.)

Mearnskirk Hospital was built to accommodate children suffering from tuberculosis, which was very prevalent in the first half of the twentieth century, flourishing in the overcrowded conditions which existed in large cities such as Glasgow. Later adult patients suffering from this disease were also admitted and benefited from rest, good diet and clean air which Mearnskirk offered. An orthopaedic unit was established as the main centre for long-stay cases in the Glasgow area and functioned until 1978.

In 1946 a surgical thoracic unit was established to deal with pulmonary tuberculosis. In the fullness of time with the decline in the incidence of the disease and the advent of effective medication the number of patients requiring surgery for tuberculosis declined, and more and more cardiac surgery was performed. In recognition of the advanced work carried out in the unit, the distinguished Society of Thoracic Surgeons of Great Britain and Ireland held their annual meeting at Mearnskirk in 1955.

By 1959 Mearnskirk Hospital had become a general hospital admitting medical and surgical patients from the Victoria Infirmary with facilities for ENT surgery and later the care of geriatric patients. In 1971 two new state of the art operating theatres were built for the cardio-thoracic unit which had become the principal referral centre for the south west of Scotland, but within a decade Greater Glasgow Health Board decided on a policy of centralisation and closed the unit. The hospital was slowly wound down and in the early 1990s was sold for residential development.

The fresh air of Mearns contrasted sharply with the pollution of great cities such as Glasgow, and exposure to the open air was an important aspect of the treatment at Mearnskirk. Patients suffering from tuberculosis and poliomyelitis often required treatment literally for years, and it was not at all uncommon to spend two or three years in hospital. Mearnskirk had its own school so that the children would not be disadvantaged educationally when they returned to their homes. The people of Newton Mearns were proud of and involved with the hospital. Alfred Ellsworth MBE was a great benefactor, and was instrumental with others in arranging for celebrities such as Judy Garland, Danny Kaye, Dorothy Lamour, Mae West and Roy Rogers (with his horse) to visit the hospital.

In 1947, 123 patients, mainly children, were admitted to Mearnskirk following the polio epidemic of that year. These children had developed muscle paralysis and their rehabilitation consisted of corrective surgery and physiotherapy, including hydrotherapy. An 'under-water exercises bath' was installed for this purpose in 1947.

In April 1940 the cruiser HMS *Sussex* had been hit by a German bomb at Yorkhill Dock. Its proximity to the Royal Hospital for Sick Children at Yorkhill led to great concern that if the ammunition on board the ship blew up the hospital would be destroyed. Accordingly, the decision was made to evacuate the 300 children and staff to Mearnskirk. The first ambulances arrived at Mearnskirk at 8 a.m. and the children had all breakfasted by 10 o'clock! During the Second World War the hospital was designated an emergency medical service centre and from 1940 until 1946 treated 30,779 service personnel and 1,810 civilians, including air raid casualties.

Greenbank House was built by a Glasgow tobacco lord, Robert Allason, in 1764, and is one of several outstanding Georgian houses in the district, other fine examples being Balgray and Capelrig. Together with its renowned garden, it was donated to the National Trust for Scotland in 1976 by the Blyth family and is today the headquarters of the Trust in the west of Scotland.

Capelrig House. It is likely that the name Capelrig is derived from 'Chapel Ridge', implying the existence of an ancient church in the area. The presence of the *circa* tenth century Capelrig Cross at nearby Holm Farm lends support to the theory that there was an early ecclesiastical presence in the area. Removed to Kelvingrove Museum in 1926, only the shaft remains. Having purchased the estate from the Mure family of Caldwell in 1765, Robert Barclay, a Glasgow lawyer, subsequently built 'a neat handsome house, three storeys high, rustic covered with eleven steps of a stone stair up to the front door' (*History of the Shire of Renfrew*, Crawford & Semple, 1782). The right wing was added in 1913. Capelrig now houses offices used by East Renfrewshire Council.

Robert Anderson left school at the age of eleven in order to help his widowed mother run the coal merchant and hauliers business which had been founded in Spiersbridge in 1832 by his grandfather, William Anderson. He was a keen cyclist and started a cycle repair business, obtaining the agency for Humber cycles in 1897. In 1900, having developed an interest in the internal combustion engine, he acquired the local agency for Humber cars and started a motor car business. Andersons garage opened in 1902 on the Kilmarnock Road just south of Newton Mearns Cross. At its height it employed over 130 people and had a training school for 25 apprentices. A branch was opened in Giffnock in 1915. Robert Anderson's house, Craigard, is seen to the left of the garage.

In 1938 the original stables and hayloft (in which eight horses could be stabled) were altered and enlarged to accommodate the used car department. It is said that the stables once accommodated an elephant from a travelling circus which was in the area. Between the wars James Anderson competed with distinction in motor rallies in his home-built 'Anderson specials', four experimental racing cars in which he developed his innovative ideas. In 1963 an article in the magazine *Sports Car* described the last of the specials (built in 1938/1939) thus: 'it represented one of the most formidable trial cars ever seen in action . . . it had an under floor flat-eight engine, four-wheel drive, interconnected hydraulic suspension, inboard brakes and dry sump lubrication – 25 years ago!'. One of the specials is on display in the Museum of Transport in Glasgow. It was driven by James Anderson in rallies and hill climbs in the 1930s, and was capable of achieving 85 m.p.h. and doing 42 miles to the gallon.

This picture of the workshop dates from 1906; the rear wheels of the chassis in the foreground are positioned over the inspection pits. In the early days the garage incorporated a blacksmith's shop, as spare parts and tools were often non-existent and had to be manufactured on the spot. The first car which Robert Anderson owned was a 10 h.p. Beeston Humber, registration HS 39, which he purchased in 1904. The first vehicle sale he made was to Mr D. M. Hannay of Broom, who purchased a 10/12 Coventry Humber for £324 14s. on 7 March 1906. The basic price of the car was £315, but extras – such as non-slip tyres at a cost of £2 8s. – were also supplied. Andersons were great innovators, and in addition to the advanced features built into the specials, the firm developed a brake testing machine and a flowline service facility – an efficient production line which allowed 50 cars to be serviced in a day. In the 1950s Maurice Anderson and Roy Hastie, the sales manager, won the Concours de Confort in the Monte Carlo rally outright, having competed many times in the late 1940s and 50s.

The showroom *c.*1924. From left to right the cars are a Humber, an Austin and a 'bullnose' Morris Cowley. The latter bears a 1924 number plate. HS was the original Renfrewshire registration.

From the early days the company bought in chassis on to which they built vehicle bodies. This picture of an ambulance built at the time of the First World War is a fine example of Andersons' engineering skills. It was the first motor ambulance in Scotland, and was supplied to the Glasgow depot in 1912.

This diorama was erected *c.*1957 outside Craigard, next to the garage, to promote the Hillman Minx.

During the Second World War the engineering side of the business was involved in munitions production. The workforce was largely female, and many local women such as those illustrated here became competent machinists. James Anderson's inventive mind was exercised in the engineering department of the garage, where he introduced novel and efficient production methods. In a letter dated 5 July 1943 the director general of ordnance factories of the Ministry of Supply wrote: 'it seems clear that an excellent

job of work has been done by yourselves in the war effort . . . The report and photographs I have bear testimony to the great initiative and ingenuity displayed in making machines suitable for the production of armament components'. James was awarded the MBE in 1944 in recognition of the firm's contribution to the war effort. The Vertimax lathe, which he patented in 1946, was probably the best known of James Anderson's inventions. It was later marketed by Charles Churchill in Birmingham. In the 1950s James established his engineering workshop at Thornliebank Industrial Estate.

The Transport Act of 1930 led to a great deal of consolidation and reorganisation in the Scottish bus industry. By 1932 various companies had been brought together to form the Western Scottish Motor Traction Company Ltd. (Western SMT), and this created the need for a new depot in the Newton Mearns area. This picture, taken at the depot in the 1930s, shows (from left to right) Hugh Ferguson (foreman mechanic), William McMillan (overnight foreman), Hugh Young (office worker), John Bell (depot manager), Thomas Melville (inspector) and William Humphries (bus driver). By the 1960s the premises were beginning to show their age and additional space was required. As extension was impractical, the decision was taken to build a replacement depot at Carnwadric Road, Thornliebank. When this opened in 1968 the Newton Mearns premises were closed. *Picture reproduced by courtesy of Mrs Agnes Melville.*

Buses were stationed at the Newton Mearns depot to serve Western's many local routes radiating south-west from Glasgow to areas such as Eaglesham, Barrhead, Neilston and Mearnskirk. Other services to Kilmarnock, Ayr and Ardrossan were also operated from there. Seen here outside the depot in the mid-1930s is a Gilford coach belonging to Western SMT with depot superintendent John Bell on the left. He had started a lifetime's work in the bus industry with O'Hara's Southern bus service of Barrhead as a driver on their service from Glasgow to Ayr via Newton Mearns and Kilmarnock. Many local people found employment in the depot as drivers, conductresses, mechanics and office workers and many Mearns folk still remember with fondness the excellent service they received as passengers.

The cattle shows of the Mearns Agricultural Society were first held in 1835 and took place annually until the 1950s. They were latterly held in Crookfur Park on the last Saturday in April, commencing at '11 o'clock prompt'. The shows caused great excitement and activity in the community. Houses in the village were whitewashed for the occasion and the local baker had to employ extra help in the week of the show in order to cater for extra demand. The cattle shows were an important aspect of rural life, and fairs such as the one pictured here were held in the evenings following them. In addition to the shows, a ploughing match was held on stiff ground at Patterton in January. Mearns Horticultural Society, founded in 1858, also had a strong local following, as did the Mearns Rose Society.

Writing in *Old Days and Ways in Newton Mearns*, published in 1939, the Revd A. Boyd Scott said of the late nineteenth century that: 'there was less leisure then, but life was more leisurely', adding that 'Pleasures were simpler and more enduring'. Although amusement was largely self-made, there were a number of popular organisations and annual events. At one time the village boasted a brass band, a pipe band, and an association called 'the Covenanters' (the modern equivalent would be the Sealed Knot Society). This picture shows a lorry from Wallace's Netherplace works decorated with pictures of Princess Margaret and Princess Anne for a gala day. The vehicle is an Austin five-tonner, probably built in 1946.

The local branch of the Royal British Legion held gala days in the post war years. This photograph of the Gala Queen of 1950, Margaret McMillan, and her attendants was taken in the public park. The following year a tragedy occurred when one of the attendants, a young boy called Gilbert Cosh, sustained a head injury when he fell off a float when a horse reared. He died a few days later.

Mearns Bowling Club was officially opened on 14 May 1921 by Arthur Gilmour of Townhead House when the photograph below was taken. The original clubhouse was a Nissen steel bow hut (on the left of the picture), purchased for the sum of £35. Townhead House is in the background.

The green of Mearns Bowling Club was laid out by Robert Provan of Rutherglen at a cost of £1,050. There were originally about 100 members in the ladies' section, a fact that was remarked upon by Mr Gilmour in his opening speech. He thought 'the club had acted wisely in admitting ladies. There was now a lady Member of Parliament, and they had ladies as Justices of the Peace, and members of the juries, and he had noticed there was a proposal to have lady deacons and elders in the Church' (*Pollokshaws News*, Friday 20 May 1921). 500 tickets were printed for the opening event.

Whitecraigs Golf Club was formally founded in July 1905, and its existence probably owes much to the establishment of the adjacent railway station (dating from *c.*1903), and the extension of the tram service from Newlands to Eastwood Toll in 1905. The course was set out on land leased from three local proprietors, primarily the Clements' estate, and was opened in May 1906 by the Lord Provost of Glasgow, Sir John Ure Primrose. The only land actually purchased at the time was that upon which the clubhouse was built. Illustrated here in its original form, the clubhouse was completed in November 1906 and was designed so that it could be converted to two private residences should the club not prosper and be wound up. Such concerns never materialised and a healthy membership existed from the start. Within a year of its formation there were over 420 'members', some 120 'lady associates' and 20 'juniors'. The club purchased the rest of the leased land in the early 1920s. (Information kindly provided from the forthcoming publication *History of The Whitecraigs Golf Club*.) In 1937 Eastwood Golf Club moved to Muirshield (its present location) from Giffnock where it had been founded in 1893.

Loganswell School was established in the 1850s in a former tollhouse situated just south of the junction of the Old Mearns Road with the Kilmarnock Road. It closed in 1928 when the pupils and their teacher transferred to Mearns School. Later it became a private residence, owned by a Mrs Jeannie Cunningham who sold refreshments to walkers and cyclists.

Other small schools in the district included a 'Leddies School' (i.e. a school run by a mistress rather than a master) in the village, and a one-room school at Polloktoun (illustrated here), with the schoolroom on the ground floor and the teacher's living accommodation above it. The last teacher was called Dominie Dunn, and the building still stands at Polloktoun.

Mearns School was built to comply with the Education Act (Scotland) of 1872 which made the education of 5–13 year olds compulsory. Despite this, an educational census in 1873 revealed that of 576 children eligible to attend school in Mearns parish, only 396 did so. The foundation stone was laid on 29 October 1875, and the school started admitting pupils almost a year later. A marble plaque records the formal opening. It reads, 'To commemorate the munificent gift of J. D. Hamilton Esq. of Greenbank to the parish of Mearns of this school, teacher's house and site at a cost of £4,575. 11th October 1878'. Mr Hamilton was chairman of the school board. The new Mearns Primary School with accommodation for over 900 pupils has recently opened. The war memorial, which was originally located at the school, was moved to its present site in the John Russell Memorial Garden on Ayr Road and rededicated on 13 November 1983.

Described in the *New Statistical Account* as 'one of the largest and airiest of any [school] in the west of Scotland', Mearns Parish School stood on the site of the present Mearnskirk Parish Church manse. In 1842 the roll consisted of 103 pupils who had the opportunity of studying Latin, geography, arithmetic, English grammar, reading and writing. The teacher's annual salary was £34 4s. although this was supplemented by school fees which amounted to £63. This school served the community until it was replaced by the new school on the Kilmarnock Road in 1875. The photograph was taken *c*.1900 by John Crawford, a keen local photographer. His trademark is his bicycle which appeared in many of his photographs. Three little boys are standing beside a well in the foreground and Mrs Reid who owned the sweetie shop at Mearnskirk is pictured cleaning the doorway of the school.

In the *Statistical Account* of 1796 the Revd George McLatchie records that 'a very good manse was built in 1789'. This was replaced in 1842 by the building illustrated here, which stands at the junction of the Old Mearns Road and Old Humbie Road. Largely obscured by trees, it has been divided in to private residences. The present manse was built in 1960 and stands on the site of the old parish school.

It is likely that there has been a church on this site in Mearnskirk since Celtic times, for it is known that there was an altar dedicated to St Bride (452–525) here. In 1273 Sir Herbert de Maxwell, Lord of Mearns, provided six merks of silver from his mills in Mearns for the endowment of an additional altar, to St Mary, and for the supply of a priest. The present church was built in 1813, although substantial alterations were made in 1932 when a vestry, session house and chancel were added to the building. This picture shows the church prior to 1932. The gateposts of the churchyard are hollow and served as sentry boxes at the time of the grave-robbers. When the Anatomy Act was passed in 1832, the risk of graves being illegally robbed to provide anatomists with corpses declined. The small building with the chimney to the right of the church is the original session house in which the elders met. Little is known about the previous church building except that the author of the *Statistical Account* notes that it had been 'fitted up in a very neat and commodious manner in 1792'. According to Professor John Wilson (Christopher North), who spent some years studying at the manse in preparation for entry to university, it had a steeple. The oak pulpit in the current church was donated by Miss Fergusson Pollok of Pollok in memory of her family, whose history extends over eight centuries.

The Red Lion Inn, an old hostelry that was once used by stagecoaches, was demolished in 1935. It was situated at Mearnskirk on the Glasgow–Kilmarnock Road (the present Old Mearns Road). The road was realigned some years ago and the site of the inn is located in what is now Kirkview Crescent. The Glasgow–Kilmarnock road via Cathcart, Clarkston and Mearnskirk was one of two routes running south from the city. The other one roughly followed the line of the Thornliebank–Stewarton Road. The former was the oldest road in the district, possibly dating from Roman times and perhaps even used by Christian missionaries travelling north from the Solway. It was improved in the 1750s following the Turnpike Act, which made financial provision for the upgrading and maintenance of roads. There was an inn, the Star and Garter, on the road between Mearnskirk and Loganswell. It is a private residence today. 'From this parish there is an excellent turnpike road of three miles to Glasgow where there is a ready money market for their great quantities of milk and butter. Their butter . . . will keep sweet for a whole year' *General View of Agriculture of the County of Renfrew*, Alexander Martin, 1794. The Red Lion was in existence by 1724 for it is recorded that an incident took place there in December that year when John Barry, a carrier from Cumbernauld, raised a toast to King James VIII (the Old Pretender) 'whereupon Robert Clark who dwelt at Kirkhill and was an elder forbye, did assault him, striking and wounding him to the effusion of blood, and all out of loyalty to King George'. When the matter was brought to court no verdict was recorded! It should be remembered that Mearns folk were anti-Jacobites.

Shawhill stood on the Old Mearns Road on the approach to Mearnskirk just north of the Red Lion Inn. In the days of stagecoaches the inhabitants of Shawhill would have been familiar with the sound of horses labouring up the steep incline to the Red Lion, where after a halt they would proceed on their way south to Ayrshire. Professor John Wilson (1785–1854) studied under the Revd George McLatchie at the Manse of Mearns in preparation for university entrance, becoming Professor of Moral Philosophy in Edinburgh in 1820. Under the pen name Christopher North, he wrote fondly of his days in Mearns and recalled the stagecoaches: 'The highflier coach! Carrying six in and twelve outside – driver and guard excluded – rate of motion eleven miles an hour with stoppages. Why, in the name of heaven, are all people nowadays in such a haste and hurry?' Professor Wilson was a satirical essayist and poet who wrote for *Blackwood's Magazine*. His great-great-great grandson is Ludovic Kennedy, the writer and broadcaster.

MEARNS KIRK

Wardhill stood on the Old Mearns Road approximately opposite Humbie Gate. The building beside the house was a little shop which sold confectionery and postcards. The bicycle propped up against its wall is likely to have been that of the photographer John Crawford. Adding captions to photographs was a difficult process which involved writing the desired text in mirror-image on the reverse of the negative, and the wording 'MEARNS KIRK' on this print is unusually neat. More frequently, handwritten captions on early photographs look much more wobbly!

Gateside Mearns

J. Crawford

The row of agricultural workers' cottages that formed Gateside was situated on the approach to Mearnskirk on the west side of the Old Mearns Road, near the present Shawwood Crescent. It was known locally as Thumble Ha' (Thimble Hall) and was demolished in the 1930s.

Robert Pollok (1798–1827) was born at North Moorhouse farm in the parish of Eaglesham. Baptised in the Secession Church at the Newton, he attended the parish school at Mearnskirk for six years and then transferred to the school at Fenwick to study Latin in preparation for entry to the University of Glasgow, where he later graduated Master of Arts. His epic poem *The Course of Time* was widely read and highly acclaimed. Fifteen months after publication by Blackwood in March 1827, the publisher reported '12,000 copies have been sold, and it is selling as fast as ever'. Pollok's *Tales of the Covenanters* had popular appeal in an area which had experienced the persecution of the Covenanters 160 years before. Licensed as a preacher in the anti-Burgher school in the spring of 1827, he died in Southampton en route to Italy in a forlorn attempt to restore his failing health. His Gothic-style granite memorial, which stands at the junction of the Old Mearns Road and the Ayr Road at Loganswell, was unveiled in the presence of a large crowd on 24 September 1900. Robert Pollok's memorial in Millbrook Cemetery, Southampton reads: 'His immortal poem is his monument'.

Mearns Castle. 'The interior of the edifice, which is still in good preservation, has in recent times been the scene of more than festive assembly. The members of the Mearns troop of Yeomen cavalry, previous to their disembodiment, held several of their annual balls within the precincts of the ancient hall, when the rank and beauty of the district graced it with their presence' *Rambles Round Glasgow*, Hugh Macdonald, 1854. The 'edifice' of Mearns Castle is a familiar landmark adjacent to Mearns Castle High School. A licence to build the castle was granted at Stirling on 8 August 1440. A second licence, given to build and fortify it, was issued on 15 March 1449. The site was well-chosen on high ground overlooking the Lac de Alton, a hollow which would have acted rather like a moat, and affording commanding views of the district stretching to the Campsies, Kilpatrick Hill and the Argyll hills. As far as is known, no military action ever took place at Mearns Castle although in 1675, 50 infantry and twelve cavalry were garrisoned at the castle with the purpose of persecuting the Covenanters. At one time conventicles were held in the castle but later the Covenanters met on the Mearns Moor, which was common land.